PERSONAL MARKET
Copyright 2013
by Andrew L. Stevans

All Rights Reserved

ISBN: 978-0-9848340-8-2
Library of Congress Cataloging-in Publication Data:

CONTACT:
P.O. Box 613, Merrifield, VA 22116-0613

1) **Personal Marketing**
2) PPM: **Planning and Personal Marketing**

CreateSpace
7920 Investment Drive, Suite B
North Charleston, SC 29418
www.CreateSpace.com

Printed in the USA

PERSONAL MARKETING

How to Sell YOU, Every Time, All the Time
The Secret of Structured Selling

By Andrew L. Stevans

INTRODUCTION

PERSONAL MARKETING
What follows is a method used to sell yourself and your ideas successfully. It teaches a technique that helps you maintain high levels of credibility in situations encountered daily.

IMPORTANT MARKETING TERMS
As in all professions, it is essential to understand the language of the profession. Personal Marketing terms are fairly straight-forward...

Closing
Asking for what you want. Examples are: a job, a loan, an order for a product or a service, a date...

Credibility
The extent to which words and actions are believable by others.

Credibility Concept
When used with empathy, this technique maintains a person's trust (also called the *Princeton Technique*).

Feature/Benefit/Response
Demonstrating exactly how your particular solution benefits the other person's need; then

awaiting their response.

Initial Benefits Statement
Showing how to resolve an individual's need/s by suggesting a preliminary, concrete solution.

Key words
A useful tool in conversation providing a way to remember factual information.

Plan of Action
The final strategy to achieve your objective, similar to a current short-term objective in planning.

Rapport
Making a positive impression in order to establish mutual trust.

Referencing
Selling an new idea (solution) by referring to a similar one that is already resolved.

Structured Selling
A highly effective selling technique.

EFFECTIVE SELLING REQUIRES EXCELLENT PERSONAL MARKETING SKILLS. THESE SKILLS CAN BE ACHIEVED THROUGH THE USE OF THE *STRUCTURED SELLING* TECHNIQUE.

A. WHAT IS STRUCTURED SELLING?

Selling may be learned using a structured approach comprised of four steps:

1. ESTABLISH RAPPORT
2. CREATE INTEREST AND ADDRESS NEED
3. GAIN REACTION AND AGREEMENT
4. CLOSE OR INITIATE A PLAN OF ACTION.

1. ESTABLISHING RAPPORT

By acting in a relaxed and friendly manner toward those we meet, we are laying the ground work for mutual trust. But we do not surrender ourselves completely. Maintaining a respectful distance and presenting ourselves in a business-like, yet supportive manner, we are recognized by others as competent, sincere and professional. The first step in determining the needs of the other party is to gain his trust and thus obtain his confidence.

KEY POINTS: ESTABLISHING RAPPORT:
--Focus completely; in sports it's called competitive concentration.
--Listen attentively; listen at least 60% of the time.

--Show interest; do not allow distractions to interfere.
--Empathize: see yourself in the listener's place.

2. CREATING INTEREST AND ADDRESSING NEED

It is necessary to earn the right to talk. To sell ourselves effectively, we must create rapport. This is an essential first step toward gaining attention and interest. Our aim is to learn (draw out) the needs of the listener and--for the purposes of Personal marketing—to address his need(s) with a solution which will be mutually beneficial.

An effective method of creating interest is **"The IBS: Initial Benefits Statements"**.

EXAMPLE: A computer salesman could make the following Initial Benefits Statement to a customer:

"If this program could <u>cut your inventory by half</u>, would you consider <u>purchasing a computer system</u>?"

EXAMPLE: To your spouse: (You're aware that the checking account is running low on funds).

"I know that you planned to shop today. Why don't we pick up a few items after the <u>movie you wanted to see</u>, and we can do <u>a major shopping on Friday</u>? It will be much easier on our checking account."

EXAMPLE: You know your manager hasn't eaten lunch. He's waiting to hear from a late client. You have your manager's trust (and in your personal plan you want his job when he's promoted). You say, "Sam, <u>go ahead and get your lunch</u>. I know your strategy with this client, and I managed his account last year. <u>I can cover for you</u> until you get back. I'll make sure he doesn't leave without talking with you."

In each example above, you are addressing a need of the other person. You are creating interest because you are talking to the other person about <u>what they want</u>. But, in addition to the good feeling you get from addressing their needs, you are also getting <u>what you want</u>.

In the first example, the computer salesman has determined that the customer has an inventory turnover problem. By providing a computer solution to the problem, the customer is getting what he wants, namely, to carry less inventory; and the salesman gets what he wants as well: the sale of a computer system and the resulting commission check.

Can you determine the "what they want" and "what you want" statements in the second and third examples, above? (<u>Underlined</u>)

<u>KEY POINT</u>: A carefully considered Initial Benefits Statement provides the listener a potential solution to their need/s.

3. GAINING REACTION AND AGREEMENT BY USING PENCIL-SELLING and REFERENCE SELLING:

An important step in selling ourselves is to elicit reaction and agreement from the other party. This is accomplished by asking an opinion, questioning openly, then asking a perfunctory,
"Don't you agree"? Press to find out what things are agreed on and what things are not.
<u>Note</u>: "Here, let me prove to you what I said was true" is the unstated message.

To gain Reaction and Agreement Pencil- Selling and Reference Selling can be effective tools.

AN EXAMPLE OF PENCIL SELLING: (avoid doodling)
Jim's an architect. He has been trying to convince his customer Hal to build two expensive fire exits which Hal knows he needs.
"Hal, we'll put both fire exits at the back of the building, where the hill is?"
Hall responds, "Yeah, yeah, I know where the hill is."
Jim continues,
"Let me sketch them into the drawings, here. There, that's exactly where they'll be. Now do you see the money saving advantage?"
Hal rubs his chin, "Well I'll be! Now I see.

The ground is closer there so we won't need those expensive steps from the second story...but I just don't see how you'll do it."

Jim smiles, "C'mon Hal, I'll buy you lunch."

In the above example, as Jim penciled in the exit doors for the fire exit, Hal began to see a more complete picture of a money saving solution to his problem. However, he's still a little shaky about making a decision. So Jim takes Hal to lunch in order to use the Apex building, a local building that's on the way to the restaurant, as a reference sell to further convince Hal.

REFERENCE SELLING

Jim knows that he and Hal will pass the site where a similar fire exit problem has been economically solved.

"Hal, see the Apex building. I'll drive down this alley. Take a look at their fire exits." Hal shades his eyes while studying the rear of the Apex Building. Suddenly he throws his hands up.

"Of course, Jim. Those doors will open onto a short ramp and then down into the parking lot. That's easy and very inexpensive. Let's do it."

ANOTHER EXAMPLE OF PENCIL SELLING (Listing)

A second method of pencil selling is to list the "positives" (the benefits to the buyer) on the left side of a piece of paper, and the "negatives" on the right side.

Jim is prepared. Below is the list that Jim could give to Hal during lunch, if needed. Note that the positives appear to outweigh the negatives:

Positives:
--Doors are cheaper to install when closer to the ground.
--No need for expensive second story metal access steps.
--Easy access to parking lot via an inexpensive ramp.
--A single ramp is used to service both doors.

Negatives:
--Must have Fire Marshall's approval. (True in either case.)
--Must have additional lighting. (An inexpensive item.)
--Ramp requires winter snow removal. (Even harder to remove snow from steps.)

GAINING REACTION AND AGREEMENT
FEATURE, BENEFIT, RESPONSE
This technique has many names. The generic name, the Feature-Benefit-Response Statement, requires that you first define a feature to the listener, then provide the feature's benefit(s), and finally, ask for the listener's agreement ("YES" or "NO" statement); or ask an "open-ended" question (WHAT, HOW, WHEN, WHERE, WHY, or

WHO) in order to determine any further objections of the other party.

EXAMPLE: 1. FEATURE, 2. BENEFIT, 3. RESPONSE
A car salesman is remarking to Betty on the car manufacturer's recommended downshifting on grades,
"Betty, you have 1) an automatic floor shift in the sports model. 2) With the automatic shift on the floor, you do not have to reach up to the steering column to down shift on a grade. In fact, you can do what many sports car drivers do: keep your right arm on the arm rest, next to the gear shift knob. 3) What are your feelings about the floor shift feature, Betty?"
Note: this is an open-ended question. That is, the question cannot be answered with a simple yes or no. Betty must express her feelings and/or her objections.

Let's review this valuable technique used to gain Reaction and Agreement. In the above example, the feature is the gearshift on the floor. Betty is accustomed to an automatic transmission with the gearshift on the steering column (and the salesman wants to sell Betty the more expensive sports car). So, he provides an attractive benefit, that of having a floor shift, and an arm rest located near to the gear shift knob. He asks an open-ended question to gain a response.

9

Note: The rule for beginning an open-ended question is to always start the sentence with a "What", "How", "When", "Where", "Why", or "Who".

HANDLING OBJECTIONS
While gaining reaction and agreement, we also have to handle objections. Regardless of how illogical or naive the objection, your response must be objective, honest, and respectful of the objecting party.

Handling objections provides the opportunity to apply role playing and empathy skills. You must put yourself in the other person's place for the moment. See his problems and needs through his eyes. (Note: At this time, you may even conclude that your party is so distracted by other problems that it would be best to arrange another meeting time.)

RULES: Maintain a role playing mode. Find a related area of agreement, if possible, in order to maintain good rapport. Restate the objection,
        "Let me see if I understand, ...". Use good eye contact. Be patient and maintain poise.

EXAMPLE: Handling Objections: In this scenario Liz is an advertising manager. You are a marketing manager. Liz is furious with you. You have forgotten to pick up a UPS order during lunch.

Two hours were set aside, starting now, to handle the UPS order and get the results back to the customer by overnight delivery. You are also aware that Liz has to leave work early. Liz glares at you as you exit the elevator empty handed. You immediately begin to role play, putting yourself in Liz's place. She's half mad at herself because she hasn't reminded you since yesterday to stop at UPS. You were doing her a favor.

NOTE: You could get defensive, or apologize, and continue on with your own busy and demanding day.

However, you respect Liz and the job she's doing. You've also strategized in your Personal Business Plan (refer to the **Introduction to PPM**, found at the end of PERSONAL MARKETING) that you want the director of marketing slot. You will need Liz's ongoing cooperation and support.

"Liz, I'm sorry. (Use eye contact. Speak sincerely and make a statement to maintain your rapport.) "I know that you want to leave early today. (Remember your own planning objective.) Consider me still at lunch. I'll go by UPS and be back in ten minutes. Liz, please cover for me if the marketing director comes looking for me." ...leave at once; don't wait for her response. (You've turned the objection around and probably made more than a few points with Liz.)

KEY POINTS:
TO OBTAIN REACTION AND AGREEMENT...
--Ask open-ended questions
--Apply the Feature, Benefit, Response approach
--Pencil Sell (list positives and negatives)
--Reference sell
--Respond to an objection with honesty; maintain respect for the objecting party.

4. CLOSING: INITIATING A PLAN OF ACTION
At a point in any selling situation, it's necessary to close the conversation. The timing of the close is important and comes with experience. But you now have gone through the three initial steps of the structured selling technique and during those steps you should have completed the execution of your selling strategy.

In this last step, you must decide when it is time to ask for the listener's business, or the favor that you wanted, or maybe the job that you have just been interviewed for perhaps you have been building up to asking that special someone to marry you. In any case, you are ready to execute The Fundamental Close.

At this point, make <u>a short summary-statement</u> and <u>ask for the order</u>; <u>say nothing more</u> until the buyer commits himself or asks another question. If your objective has been met, that is, if you have successfully closed, you thank him for his business, reaffirm your promises and gracefully make your exit. However, if you must answer another question or objection, <u>answer patiently</u> and again <u>ask for the order</u>. <u>Quietly wait for the buyer to commit himself</u>.

If the give and take continues, it may be necessary to tactfully question if the person is able to make the decision on his own. At this time you may want to make sure you are selling to the correct individual.

Frequently it isn't possible to obtain total commitment to your ideas or product. When this happens you must establish a future time to discuss differences and to again attempt to close the situation to your complete advantage. Tact and tenacity are extremely important to a successful close.

<u>KEY POINTS</u>:
--A Close may be attempted at any time during Structured Selling.
--The timing of the close comes with practice and is often the obvious next step in a negotiation.
--Once you ask for the order or make the request, say nothing. Quietly await a response.
--The ABC's of selling: <u>A</u>lways <u>B</u>e <u>C</u>losing.
--Real selling begins when the other party says "no!"

B. HOW TO MAINTAIN CREDIBILITY
(a.k.a. *The Princeton Technique)*

According to the American Heritage Dictionary, a "credible" person is believable, worthy of trust. Maintaining credibility has been emphasized throughout the structured sales technique. In the "rapport" step, it is described as being sincere and promoting a mutual trust. In the "creating interest" step, it is earning the right to talk. In the "handling objections" section, it is described as being objective, honest, showing respect.

There is probably no shortcut way to earn and keep your credibility with others. It requires vigilance and integrity at all times. But there is a method used in interviewing which comes close. It's called the "Princeton Technique". The origins are vague but possibly it was included as part of a kinesics (body language) class at Princeton.

To summarize the technique, when you are asked an open-ended question, or you are in a conversation where you need to respond, pause, then attempt to answer completely in about 15 seconds. The technique requires the following steps:

1. Restate the question if it is vague or

misleading. If you must restate a question, obtain agreement on the question's content.

2. If the questioner asks for your agreement or disagreement, <u>agree or disagree</u> at this point. The listener must know where you stand.

3. Within thirty seconds answer the question with one or more <u>keyword sentences</u>. The key word(s) is memorized from the question itself (example below).

4. Summarize with a brief statement relating a <u>personal ability or achievement</u>. This should only be done if the timing seems appropriate and the statement enhances your image.

EXAMPLE (Listening for key words):
Jill has just explained to a <u>non-computer</u> oriented personnel staffer that all of her experience is in <u>business systems</u> design. She further explained that she was a business and communications major at Penn State. The interviewer quickly looks over Jill's resume. "I see an impressive <u>grade point average</u> here, but I don't see the <u>degree</u>. What kind of engineer are you, Jill?"

Note: Jill could have become defensive and responded, "I mentioned earlier that I design accounting systems. I'm a systems analyst not an engineer. Engineers do not typically design business systems". Any astute interviewer would pick up on her tenseness and most likely blame it on an attitude problem. END OF INTERVIEW...

Instead, using the Princeton Technique that she learned from a corporate guest speaker at the university, Jill remembered some key words. She heard "grade point average" and "degree". She was also thinking of her own key words "computer" and "business systems". This stopped her earlier tense (and emotional) response from ever happening. Instead, Jill pauses for a moment then responds to the memorized key words. Jill's objective comment went:

"I did do well in my double major in business and communications. It was a tough curriculum at Penn State. That's how I became interested in computers. When my money ran out, I was thirty credits short of my degree. But I do have all required credits in my two major concentrations (15 seconds). Do you know that I actually helped set up the Penn State online Personnel Information and Skills Inventory computer systems? I'll finish up my degree this year, here, at the University of Rochester."

Note: Jill's response is a bit long, but she decided that a personal ability or achievement statement was essential in her interview.

Good, Jill! Every personnel staffer should know what a Personnel Information system is. What a door opener.

KEY POINTS: (There are several immediate advantages when using this credibility technique)
--You are following a structure, so, there is less tendency to digress or to wander off on a tangent during a response.
--In the mind of the listener, your responses appear organized and well thought out.
--You come across as sincere, objective and capable.

NOTES: PERSONAL MARKETING

_____

_____

_____

_____

_____

_____

_____

From the book…

PPM: PLANNING and PERSONAL MARKETING

AN INTRODUCTION

PLANNING TOMORROW'S EXCELLENCE, TODAY…

FORMAL BUSINESS AND PERSONAL PLANS FOR THE 21ST CENTURY

If the past 35 years are any indicator, it is reasonable to believe that electronic innovation will continue to grow at an ever increasing rate. The quickening pace places a great deal of added stress on the employee to remain up-to-date in the technology and, at the same time, this quickly changing technology directly impacts the organization's need to remain competitive in the marketplace. Creating an organization-wide Planning Standard can aid significantly in both areas.

THE RATIONALE FOR A STANDARD PLANNING METHODOLOGY

How does a Standardized Planning Methodology relieve employee stress and at the same time help the organization maintain its competitive edge? The answer is two-fold: First, a Planning Standard helps focus the staff by providing each individual with an accurately defined and detailed series of achievable short-term objectives. Second, it provides a common planning approach and a common planning language, used, not only throughout the organization, but in an employees Personal Life Planning as well.

COMPREHENSIVE PLANNING –
COMBINED BUSINESS AND PERSONAL PLANS

The concept of Comprehensive Planning is not new. Back in the 1960's Dick Wilson, the first president and CEO of Xerox, required both business and personal planning by his top management. By the late 1960's Xerox had a computerized system developed to inventory employee skills, much like Xerox inventoried interchangeable copier parts. Even though IBM picked up the Skills Inventory part of Wilson's plan, unfortunately, his ideas in Comprehensive Planning did not spread across the country like so many Xerox products did.

Now, in our hectic 21st century, there appears to be a resurgence of interest in Comprehensive Planning. More recently, the CEO of a thriving Texas-based Information Technology services company was asked why he required his employees to establish steps (short-term) to achieve personal (long-term) objectives. His response was, "When people feel successful in the rest of their lives, they're more apt to be successful in the workplace." Allowing the employee training time to produce personal objectives is equally beneficial to the organization.

PLANNING QUESTIONS THAT ORGANIZATIONS MUST ANSWER FIRST
Ask any large company CEO if he maintains a computerized, corporate-wide plan for the business, and most likely the answer would be an immediate, "of course!" Then ask if the corporate plan is "plugged into" every level of the organization. Does each manager and each employee understand the organization's (or even their division's or department's) long and short-term objectives? And, can each employee identify their personal effort within the organization's long-term plan?

ADVANTAGES OF FORMALIZED COMPREHENSIVE PLANNING
There are a host of reasons for organizations to give top-priority to an employee training course in comprehensive planning concepts using a Planning Standard. They include the following:

- Plans act as controllers, freeing the individual's (and thus the organization's) energies for creative growth.
- Since both home (personal) and work (business) activities follow the same planning standard, employees feel connected 24-hours a day, seven days a week. This feeling improves attitude and increases performance.
- A greater confidence is demonstrated on the job.
- There is less harmful day-to-day stress both at home and at work.

A QUICK REVIEW OF FORMAL PLANNING

The formal planning process follows several logical phases of development. Each phase will be investigated to some depth later.

Defining the Long-Term Objective is not as easy as it sounds. For example, the organization must first define its basic socio-economic purpose, the values and philosophy of management, and the organization's strengths and weaknesses. Similarly, the individual must define past achievements, their beliefs and values (what motivates them), and their personal strengths and weaknesses.

The "model" or approach used to assist in identifying these essentials needed to create a Long-Term Objective is called the BSM or "Basic Success Model."

The time taken to accurately define the BSM will greatly impact the Long-Term Objective, and, in fact, bring the short-term objectives into crystal-clear focus.

Developing a Standard Glossary of Terms

Learning and implementing a <u>Standard Planning Terminology</u> for tracking both business and personal short-term objectives achieves two immediate results. First, a standard planning vocabulary provides instant understanding of the planning process, from the CEO down to the first-line employee. Second, it provides a built-in, pro-active, management-by-objectives capability that eases the job of managing (directing/controlling).

Creating Short-Term objectives

Once a Long-Term Objective is determined, four steps are taken to successfully achieve the Long-Term Objective.
--First, list all Short-Term Objectives required to
   reach the Long-Term Objective. Place the
   Short-Term Objectives in a logical order.
--Second, Track the first (current) Short-Term
   Objective using proper format and terminology.
--Third, execute the current Short-Term
   Objective.
--Finally: Review and Evaluate the results
   against the Long-Term Objective. Then, based
   on this information, create tracking for the
   next Short-Term Objective.

A Proposed Tracking Standard: The *Quick-View Graph*

Within businesses, the Short-Term Objectives typically contain time and cost (also called Plan Dependent) information. Many non-businesses as well as personal applications contain other Plan Dependent information that must be tracked. Training for the Olympics provides an example of a long-term, time dependent effort, only. Of course training cost can easily be integrated into the plan. Time dependent... Complex physical training programs can span years, yet peak conditioning is required for an event at a specific future date.

The job of the **Quick-View Graph** is to magnify a Current Short-Term objective. A Short-Term Objective is comprised of a series of activities (strategies) that are required to assure success. Tracking is accomplished by creating a prioritized list of strategies. A horizontal Tracking Calendar reflects the numbered priorities.

PPM SUMMARY

A PLANNED ODYSSEY...

Without formal written or computerized plans, a standardized vocabulary and an easy to use methodology to track current short-term strategies, objectives are frequently out of focus. Guess work results. Project may become vague and ultimately unrealistic. Unstudied, careless planning closely parallels the definition of the word *odyssey:* "random wanderings with changing fortunes."

Good planning can be viewed as a *planned odyssey. A* definition might be: "carefully planned strategies with predictable successes." Using *ODYSSEY* as an acronym, the following may assist in remembering the steps to proper planning...

Objective: A statement describing achievable long or short-term results.

Destiny: A predetermined series of short-term objectives that achieve predictable, long-term results.

You: (Or your management's) beliefs and values: the driving force within a plan's infrastructure.

Strategies: Activities numbered by priority and producing predictable, short-term results.

Steps: The process necessary to build a Quick-View-Graph for each current, short-term objective while progressing toward the long-term result

Execute: Implementing the strategies (activities) necessary to achieve predictable, current, short-term results.

Yield: Results following proper execution.

NOTE: Review and evaluate each current short-term objective used to achieve a long-term result.

If we take a little time today to develop written, integrated business and personal plans, raw ambition will quickly become realistic achievements, and tomorrow's success will be assured.

GLOSSARY OF TERMS
PPM: Planning and Personal Marketing

(NOTE: *Underlined Terms are used in <u>Personal Marketing</u>*)

Activities
The actions needed to achieve a current, short-term objective.

Basic Success Model
A well defined framework for Personal Planning.

Business Plan
A formalized (written) set of procedures designed to achieve a business objective.

<u>Closing</u>
Finalizing the request by asking for what you want. Examples are: a job, a loan, an order for a product or a service, a date...

<u>Credibility</u>
The extent to which words and actions are believable by others.

<u>Credibility Concept</u>
A technique which, when used with empathy, establishes and maintains a person's trust (also called the *Princeton Technique*).

Feature/Benefit/Response
Demonstrating exactly how your particular
solution benefits a person's need; then awaiting
their response.

Initial Benefits Statement
Showing how to resolve an individual's need/s by
suggesting a preliminary, concrete solution.

Interview for Objective
A priority setting interview method, used in
Personal planning.

Key words
A useful tool in conversation providing a way to
remember factual information.

Long term (abbrev: **LT**)
A period of time, typically longer than six months.

Objective
The goal, also known as the mission or project.

Personal Plan
A formalized set of procedures designed to achieve
a personal life objective.

Plan
A formalized (written) set of procedures tailored to
an individual or a business.

Plan of Action
The final strategy to achieve your selling objective, similar to a current short-term objective in planning.

Plan Dependent Information
Everything (the steps, activities, time phasing, etc) that comprises the current, short-term plan.

Planning Cycle
One review-period within a plan's short-term efforts.

Prioritize
Creating a chronological list of activities that will result in achieving a short-term objective.

(The) Princeton Technique
A Personal Marketing technique used to maintain credibility.

Quick-View Graph
The graph provides a snap shot of dates, times, prioritized activities and tracking needed to achieve a current short-term objective.

Rapport
Making a positive impression in order to establish mutual trust.

Referencing (Reference Selling)
Selling an new idea (solution) by referring to a similar one that is already resolved.

Review and Evaluation
A periodic check of a plan's *Quick-View Graphs* to assure accuracy and success of a current short-term objective.

Short term (abbrev: ST)
A plan's current activities designed to successfully work toward the long-term objective

Short-Term Objective
One step toward achieving a long-term objective.

Strategy
A series of prioritized activities in the current short-term objective.

Steps
Providing an sequence to short-term objectives, in order to provide an easy way to refer to and track all short-term objectives.

Strategic Planning
Devising the best approach to achieve an objective, either short or long-term.

Structured Selling
A highly effective selling technique.

Andrew Stevans writes in Northern Virginia. He graduated from George Mason University with a double major in Computer Science and Business Management, and graduate studies in Human Resource Management and Law.

He has worked as a farm hand, a Navy petty-officer, a computer-systems engineer, an adult-ed instructor, a staffing manager, a lecturer and a personnel consultant.

P. O. Box 613, Merrifield, VA 22116-0613

www.ingramcontent.com/pod-product-compliance
Lightning Source LLC
Chambersburg PA
CBHW070749210326
41520CB00016B/4644